Check Your
Egos at the Door

Doonesbury books by G. B. Trudeau

Still a Few Bugs in the System
The President Is a Lot Smarter Than You Think
But This War Had Such Promise
Call Me When You Find America
Guilty, Guilty, Guilty!
"What Do We Have for the Witnesses, Johnnie?"
Dare To Be Great, Ms. Caucus
Wouldn't a Gremlin Have Been More Sensible?
"Speaking of Inalienable Rights, Amy . . ."
You're Never Too Old for Nuts and Berries
An Especially Tricky People
As the Kid Goes for Broke
Stalking the Perfect Tan
"Any Grooming Hints for Your Fans, Rollie?"
But the Pension Fund Was Just Sitting There
We're Not Out of the Woods Yet
A Tad Overweight, but Violet Eyes to Die For
And That's My Final Offer!
He's Never Heard of You, Either
In Search of Reagan's Brain
Ask for May, Settle for June
Unfortunately, She Was Also Wired for Sound
The Wreck of the "Rusty Nail"
You Give Great Meeting, Sid
Doonesbury: A Musical Comedy

In Large Format
The Doonesbury Chronicles
Doonesbury's Greatest Hits
The People's Doonesbury
Doonesbury Dossier: The Reagan Years

a Doonesbury book by

GB Trudeau.

Check Your Egos at the Door

An Owl Book Holt, Rinehart and Winston / New York

The author and publisher gratefully acknowledge
the following companies that contributed time and material
to make this book possible:
Abington Display Company, Inc.; Alling and Cory;
Color Associates, Inc.; The Lehigh Press, Inc.;
Phoenix Color Corporation.

Published by Holt, Rinehart and Winston,
383 Madison Avenue, New York, New York 10017.

Published simultaneously in Canada by Holt, Rinehart and
Winston of Canada, Limited.

Library of Congress Catalog Card Number: 85-80634

ISBN: 0-03-005627-6

First Edition

Printed in the United States of America

The cartoons in this book have appeared in newspapers
in the United States and abroad under the auspices of
Universal Press Syndicate.

1 3 5 7 9 10 8 6 4 2

ISBN 0-03-005627-6

OKAY, THIS IS JUST ONE POSSIBILITY. I THOUGHT I'D TRY TO PLAY UP HIS MANLY IMAGE WITH A SURREAL, VIDEO APPROACH..

GOOD DIRECTION!

WE OPEN ON A ROCK CONCERT WITH A MULTI-RACIAL BAND PLAYING IN FRONT OF A HUGE AMERICAN FLAG. AS BLINDING FIREWORKS ERUPT, THE FLAG LIFTS TO REVEAL A LONG, WHITE STAIRCASE! \

STANDING AT THE TOP IS REAGAN. HE'S DRESSED IN JEANS AND AN OPEN SHIRT. AS A THOUSAND TEENAGERS SCREAM "PEACE THROUGH STRENGTH," HE STARTS DOWN THE STAIRS.

SUDDENLY, HIS HAIR CATCHES FIRE.

BUT HE DOESN'T FLINCH! LOVE IT!

YOU KNOW, I ALWAYS *THOUGHT* HIS HAIR LOOKED FLAMMABLE.

©B Trudeau

GOOD EVENING. VICE PRESIDENT GEORGE BUSH'S MANHOOD PROBLEM SURFACED AGAIN TODAY, AS CONCERN OVER HIS LACK OF POLITICAL COURAGE CONTINUED TO GROW.

CAMPAIGN OFFICIALS, ALARMED BY REACTION TO BUSH'S NUMEROUS POLICY REVERSALS, HAVE PERSUADED HIM TO TAKE SWIFT ACTION TO PREVENT FURTHER EROSION OF HIS INTEGRITY.

ACCORDINGLY, IN A WHITE HOUSE CEREMONY TODAY, BUSH WILL FORMALLY PLACE HIS EMBATTLED MANHOOD IN A BLIND TRUST.

IT WILL BE RESTORED TO HIM ONLY IN TIMES OF NATIONAL EMERGENCY.

GB Trudeau

MR. BUSH, WHY DID YOU DECIDE TO PLACE YOUR MANHOOD IN A BLIND TRUST INSTEAD OF SOMEWHERE ELSE?

WELL, IT WAS REALLY THE PRESIDENT'S IDEA. HE'S VERY MUCH IN CONTROL OF THIS WONDERFUL ADMINISTRATION, AND I RESPECT AND ADMIRE HIM FOR IT!

WHERE TO KEEP THE VICE PRES-IDENT'S MANHOOD IS JUST ONE OF THE TOUGH DECISIONS A PRESIDENT HAS TO MAKE. LBJ, FOR INSTANCE, USED TO KEEP HUBERT HUMPHREY'S MAN-HOOD IN HIS POCKET.

DID MR. REAGAN CONSIDER THAT?

YES, BUT WE AGREED A BLIND TRUST WAS MORE DIGNIFIED.

GO AHEAD, ZONKER. TELL J.J. WHAT YOU JUST TOLD ME.

J.J., YOUR WORRIES ARE OVER. I'VE DECIDED TO GO TO MED SCHOOL.

UH-HUH. AND I'M JOINING THE BOLSHOI.

I'M SERIOUS, J.J. —I'VE APPLIED TO THE BABY DOC COLLEGE OF PHYSICIANS, THE FINEST NEW MED SCHOOL IN ALL OF HAITI!!

AND I DON'T WANT TO SOUND COCKY OR ANYTHING, BUT I HAVE EVERY REASON TO BELIEVE THAT I'M A SHOO-IN!

GB Trudeau

I DON'T KNOW, SIR. I'VE NEVER SEEN GRADES LIKE THESE.

I DON'T CARE, DEAN HONEY. WE NEED HIM TO SHORE UP THE VOLLEYBALL SQUAD!

WE BETTER HURRY, SIR. THE MAYOR OF PORT-AU-PRINCE IS ALREADY HERE TO SWEAR YOU IN!

HE CAN WAIT. I PAY HIM ENOUGH. HAS THE INAUGURATION SPEAKER SHOWED YET?

YES, SIR. LATE LAST NIGHT. A CIGARETTE BOAT DROPPED HIM OFF AT THE MARINA.

THAT SOUNDS LIKE BOBBY, ALL RIGHT..

EVER SINCE WE ROOMED TOGETHER IN COLLEGE, BOBBY'S ALWAYS HATED BEING THE CENTER OF ATTENTION.

SIR, WHO EXACTLY IS ROBERT VESCO?

KIND OF A CARIBBEAN JOHN DE LOREAN. THE KIDS WILL EAT HIM UP!

I DON'T KNOW, RICK. WITH A BLOW-OUT LIKE REAGAN'S, IT'S HARD TO FIND A SILVER LINING. I FEEL LIKE I'VE TOTALLY WASTED THE LAST THREE YEARS OF MY LIFE!

HEY, C'MON, DUANE, YOU WERE RESPONSIBLE FOR SOME MAJOR THEMATIC BREAKTHROUGHS THIS ELECTION! LIKE FERRARO! THAT WAS A VERY GUTSY CHOICE!

YOU TOOK A GREEN, BRASSY NO-NAME FROM QUEENS AND MADE HER ONE OF THE MOST IMPORTANT SYMBOLS OF THE DECADE!

YEAH. IF ONLY SHE HADN'T BEEN A WOMAN.

YOU MEAN, YOU.. YOU CHOSE HER ON HER MERITS?

HEY, HER FILE SAID "GERRY." I FIGURED A GUY.

GB Trudeau

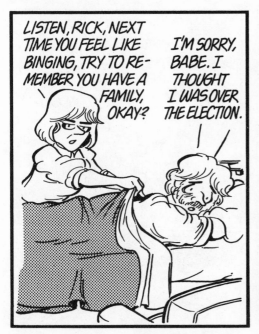

YOU MARK?

THAT'S RIGHT. WHO ARE YOU?

I'M SPANKY LEE JAMES. I'M THE ENGINEER ON YOUR NEW SHOW. WELCOME TO NPR.

HERE'S THE DEAL. AT THIS HOUR OF THE NIGHT, WE HAVE A SMALL BUT DEVOTED CALL-IN AUDIENCE. THEY ARE EDDIE, MEL, ROSITA, COL. HARWOOD, AND SOME GUY NAMED "CHICKENBONE" FROM CHICAGO.

THAT'S IT?

PRETTY MUCH. IF EDDIE CALLS, TRY TO KEEP HIM OFF J. EDGAR HOOVER.

GBTrudeau

BOOPSIE, WITH YOUR FILM CAREER TAKING OFF AND WITH B.D. PLAYING FOR THE RAMS, YOU TWO WOULD SEEM TO HAVE IT MADE. ARE YOU HAPPY?

HAPPY? I THINK SO. WHAT DO YOU MEAN?

WELL, OFTEN THERE'S A DARK UNDERSIDE TO FAME, A KIND OF DESPERATE NEED FOR MORE AND MORE ATTENTION. IT'S WHAT'S BEEN CALLED THE FAILURE OF SUCCESS.

OH.. HOLD ON A SEC, OKAY?

B.D., ARE WE HAPPY?

DEPENDS. IS THAT YOUR AGENT?

GBTrudeau

AS PARKS GO, RON, LAFAYETTE IS PROBABLY STILL THE BEST FOR STREET PEOPLE. IT'S SAFE, IT'S GOT A PUBLIC WASHROOM, AND THE AREA'S GOOD FOR PANHANDLING.

WHO'S THAT OLD GUY OVER THERE?

THAT'S CRAZY ELMONT. HE'S PRETTY HARD CORE.

HEY! OUR $200 BILLION DEFICIT CAN BE WIPED OUT WITHOUT RAISING TAXES OR CUTTING DEFENSE! HEY, LISTEN TO ME!

HOW SAD.

THE TRAGIC PRICE OF DEINSTITUTION-ALIZATION, ROB.

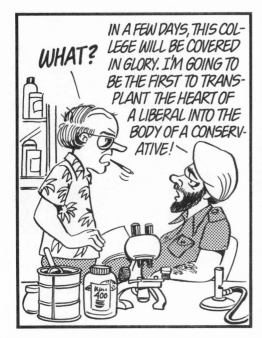

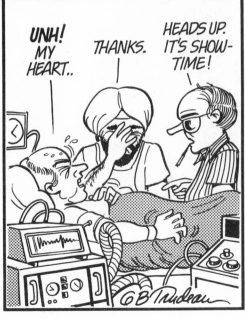

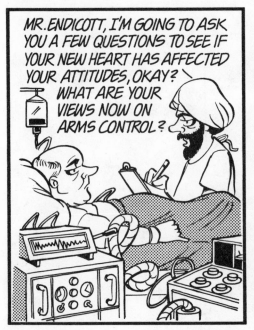

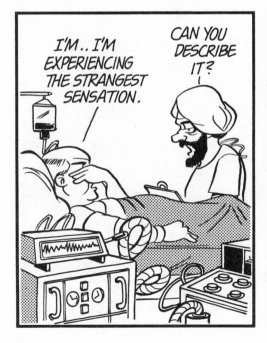

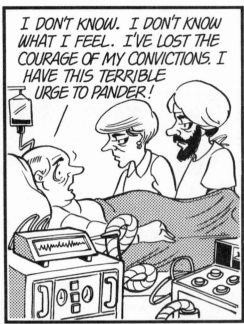